FRANCHISING IN BURUNDI 2014

Legal and Business Considerations

I0042086

KENDAL H. TYRE, JR., EXECUTIVE EDITOR
DIANA VILMENAY-HAMMOND, MANAGING EDITOR
COURTNEY L. LINDSAY II, ASSISTANT EDITOR

LEXNOIR FOUNDATION

FIRST QUARTER 2014

LexNoir Foundation is the charitable, educational arm of LexNoir, an international network of lawyers connecting the African Diaspora.

This publication, *Franchising in Burundi 2014: Legal and Business Considerations*, contains excerpts from *Franchising in Africa 2014: Legal and Business Considerations*. Both works are published by LexNoir Foundation and reflect the points of view of the authors and editors as of the date of publication and do not necessarily represent the opinions, interpretations, or positions of the law firms or organizations with which they are affiliated, nor the opinions, interpretations or positions of LexNoir Foundation or LexNoir.

Nothing contained in this book is to be considered as the rendering of legal advice, either generally or in connection with any specific issues or case. Readers are responsible for obtaining advice from their own legal counsel or other professional. This book, any forms and agreements or other information herein are intended for educational and informational purposes only.

© 2014 LexNoir Foundation. All rights reserved.

www.lexnoir.org

Table of Contents

Franchising in Burundi

Gilbert Nyatanyi and René-Claude Madebari
ENSafrica | Burundi

i

Bibliography of International Franchise Resources

Kendal H. Tyre, Jr., Diana Vilmenay-Hammond, Pierce Haesung Han, Courtney L. Lindsay II, and Keri McWilliams
Nixon Peabody LLP

Acknowledgment

This book could not have been written without the hard work and dedication of each of the contributing authors and editors. Thank you.

We would like to acknowledge and extend our heartfelt gratitude to Michael Collier and Maria Stallings of the Washington, D.C. office of Nixon Peabody LLP for their invaluable assistance in revising, proofing, and editing this publication.

About the Editors and Authors

Kendal H. Tyre, Jr. – Kendal is a partner in the Washington, D.C. office of Nixon Peabody LLP. He handles domestic and cross-border transactions, including mergers and acquisitions, joint ventures, strategic alliances, licensing, and franchise matters.

In his franchise and licensing practice, Kendal counsels domestic and international franchisors, franchisees, licensors, licensees and distributors regarding U.S. state and federal franchise laws as well as foreign franchise legislation in a variety of jurisdictions. Kendal drafts and provides advice with regard to franchise and license agreements, disclosure documents and area development agreements and has extensive experience drafting and negotiating a variety of other commercial agreements. His client base spans the United States and foreign countries, including South Africa, Kenya, and the United Kingdom.

Kendal is a frequent contributor to franchise publications and a frequent speaker at franchise programs held by the American Bar Association Forum on Franchising and the International Franchise Association.

Kendal is co-chair of the firm's Diversity Action Committee and its Africa Group. Kendal is also the executive director of LexNoir Foundation.

E-mail address: ktyre@nixonpeabody.com

Diana Vilmenay-Hammond – Diana is an attorney in the Washington, D.C. office of Nixon Peabody LLP. She is a member of the firm's Franchise & Distribution Team.

In her franchise practice, Diana works with domestic and international franchisors on transactional and litigation matters. Specifically, she counsels franchisor clients regarding state and federal franchise laws, disclosure and registration obligations.

Diana drafts and negotiates various commercial agreements, including international franchise and development agreements.

Diana has co-authored numerous articles on franchising and frequently co-hosted the Nixon Peabody franchise law webinar series. Topics have included:

- "Franchise Case Law Round-Up: Implications for Your Franchise," February 15, 2012;
- "Social Media Part II: Best Practices in Protecting Your Brand in the New Media," September 14, 2010; and
- "The Awuah Case: Bellwether or Outlier," May 11, 2010

Diana received her J.D. from Howard University School of Law and her B.A. from Georgetown University. She is a member of the American Bar Association (Forum on Franchising).

Email address: dvilmenay@nixonpeabody.com

Pierce Haesung Han – Pierce is an associate in Nixon Peabody's Global Business & Transactions Group. Pierce focuses his practice on three main areas, assisting clients with a variety of complex business transactions.

- Mergers & Acquisitions: Providing assistance to both public and private clients with various mergers and acquisitions, performing due diligence, drafting and negotiating transaction documents, and facilitating closing and post-closing mechanics.
- International Commercial Transactions: Drafting and negotiating a variety of commercial agreements, including international franchise and development agreements, license agreements, and purchase and sale agreements.
- Federal Securities Law Matters: Assisting public and private clients regarding federal securities laws and stock exchange rules relating to corporate governance and disclosure.

Pierce serves as the Secretary of the Asian Pacific Bar Association Educational Fund (an affiliate of the Asian Pacific American Bar Association of the Greater Washington, D.C. Area).

Pierce received his J.D. from Georgetown University Law Center and his B.A. from Case Western Reserve University. He is admitted to practice in the State of New York and the District of Columbia.

E-mail address: phan@nixonpeabody.com

Courtney L. Lindsay, II – Courtney is an associate in Nixon Peabody's Corporate and Finance practice. In his corporate practice, Courtney assists for-profit and non-profit entities with transactional matters and corporate governance. In various capacities, Courtney has been involved in multiple merger and acquisition transactions, including drafting and managing due diligence.

Previously, Courtney worked in the legal and business affairs department at a national cable network, where he handled matters related to the network's LLC agreement, including drafting board and member consent agreements.

Courtney received his J.D. from the University of Virginia School of Law and his B.A. from the University of Virginia. He is admitted to practice in the Commonwealth of Virginia and the District of Columbia.

E-mail address: clindsay@nixonpeabody.com

Keri McWilliams – Keri is an associate in the Franchise & Distribution team of Nixon Peabody LLP. Keri works with clients on a number of franchising issues, including obtaining and maintaining franchise registrations in various states, responding to state inquiries regarding trade practices, ongoing compliance with state and federal regulations, and updating franchise disclosure documents. She also handles franchise sales counseling and franchise system issues.

Keri is a member of the American Bar Association's Forum on Franchising, and the Federal and Minnesota State bar associations. She is also a member of Minnesota Women Lawyers and the Minnesota Association of Black Lawyers, and a volunteer in the Volunteer Lawyers Network.

Keri received her J.D. from the Georgetown University Law Center and her B.F.A. from Washington University. She is admitted to practice in the District of Columbia and Minnesota.

E-mail address: kmcwilliams@nixonpeabody.com

René-Claude Madebari – René is an associate advocate at ENSafrica | Burundi. He practices in Burundi and specializes in public procurement, corporate law, banking and finance law. He has published a number of articles and presentations and was a contributor to Doing Business 2013, in association with the International Finance Corporation and the World Bank.

René received a LLB from the Université Lumière de Bujumbura in 2009. He is a member of the Burundian Bar and the East African Law Society and is fluent in English, French, Kirundi and Swahili.

E-mail address: rmadebari@ensafrica.com

Gilbert Nyatanyi – Gilbert heads up ENSafrica | Burundi and is an executive at ENS. He has more than 15 years' experience in general legal advice and more than 10 years' solid experience in banking and finance law. He practices in Burundi and specializes in secured transactions, acquisition and corporate finance, syndicated loans, capital markets. He has acted for several companies, financial institutions and governments on a wide range of legal matters in Europe and Africa (especially the United Republic of Tanzania, the Democratic Republic of Congo, the Central African Republic, Rwanda and Burundi), and has an extensive high level network on the African continent. Gilbert's practice experience includes advising several international clients in connection with assets financing, credit transactions, mergers and acquisitions, secured transactions.

Gilbert has a Masters of Law (1995) from the University of Ghent (Belgium) and is fluent in English, French, Dutch, German and Kinyarwanda. Gilbert is recognized as a leading lawyer by the following reputable rating agency and its publication: Chambers and Partners Global Guide to the World's Leading Lawyers 2012 and 2013 – General Business Law (Burundi); and 2013 General Business Law (Burundi) (South Africa).

E-mail address: gnyatanyi@ensafrica.com

About the Book

Franchising in Burundi 2014: Legal and Business Considerations contains excerpts from the larger work, *Franchising in Africa 2014: Legal and Business Considerations*. Both books serve as practical, succinct, easy-to-use reference tools for lawyers, business people and academics to use in navigating the myriad laws and business issues impacting franchise arrangements on the African continent.

This book provides an overview of the franchise industry in Burundi and addresses the typical legal issues confronted when expanding a franchise system in Burundi. The larger work, *Franchising in Africa 2014: Legal and Business Considerations*, covers those laws governing franchising in fifteen other African countries – Angola, Botswana, Cape Verde, Democratic Republic of Congo, Egypt, Ethiopia, Ghana, Kenya, Mozambique, Nigeria, Rwanda, South Africa, Tunisia, Zambia and Zimbabwe.

In both books, an author, who is a legal expert in the designated jurisdiction, addresses the basic questions that a franchise lawyer would need to know to competently represent a client in expanding their franchise system to that country.

Each country chapter organizes a discussion of that country's laws under various headings and in a uniform format. Topics were sent to each country's author in the form of a questionnaire, and each author drafted responses to the questions presented. A general overview relating to the political and economic history of the country at the beginning of each chapter provides an initial context for the regulatory framework. [1]

---

[1] The source of information for these sections is the Central Intelligence Agency, https://www.cia.gov/library/publications/the-world-factbook/ (last visited November 3, 2013).

Apart from an overview of the legal framework for franchising, each book contains other articles and resources that should prove useful to those in the franchise industry.

The authors for each chapter are listed at the beginning of a chapter and their biographical information is listed in the previous section, *About the Editors and Authors*.

Readers should always consult with local counsel in the relevant jurisdiction instead of relying solely on the information contained in this book. The laws governing franchising are evolving and local counsel in Burundi are best positioned to provide timely, relevant advice applying the current law to the particular facts of a case.

Franchising in Burundi

Gilbert Nyatanyi and René-Claude Madebari

ENSafrica | Burundi

Bujumbura, Burundi

Burundi

I.   Introduction

A.   Historical Background of Country

Burundi's first democratically elected president was assassinated in October 1993 after only 100 days in office, triggering widespread ethnic violence between Hutu and Tutsi factions. More than 200,000 Burundians perished during the conflict that spanned almost a dozen years. Hundreds of thousands of Burundians were internally displaced or became refugees in neighboring countries. An internationally brokered power-sharing agreement between the Tutsi-dominated government and the Hutu rebels in 2003 paved the way for a transition process that led to an integrated defense force, established a new constitution in 2005, and elected a majority Hutu government in 2005. The government of President Pierre Nkurunziza, who was reelected in 2010, continues to face many political and economic challenges.

B.   Economy of the Country

Burundi's economy is predominantly agricultural; agriculture accounts for just over 30% of GDP and employs more than 90% of the population. Burundi's primary exports are coffee and tea, which account for 90% of foreign exchange earnings, though exports are a relatively small share of GDP. Burundi's export earnings - and its ability to pay for imports rests primarily on weather conditions and international coffee and tea prices. Burundi will remain heavily dependent on aid from bilateral and multilateral donors - foreign aid represents 42% of Burundi's national income, the second highest rate in Sub-Saharan Africa. Burundi joined the East African Community in 2009, which should boost Burundi's regional trade ties, and also in 2009 received $700 million in debt relief.

C.   Franchise Legal Overview

Under Burundian law, there is no specific law that regulates franchise agreements and/or transactions. The franchise agreement is seen as a contractual agreement between the parties and thus contract law will govern such an agreement.

II.   Regulatory Requirements

A.   Pre-Sale Disclosure

Please describe any pre-sale franchise disclosure or similar requirements that may apply to franchise transactions.

No pre-sale franchise disclosure or similar requirements apply to franchise transactions under the laws of Burundi.

B.   Governmental Approvals, Registrations, Filing Requirements

Please describe any necessary government approvals, registrations, or filing requirements that may apply to franchise transactions.

Local law does not provide that the effectiveness of a franchise transaction is dependent on any formalities beyond the execution of a written contract, such as government approvals, registration or filing requirements.

C.   Limits of Fees and Typical Term of Franchise Agreement

Please describe any limits upon the nature and extent of fees and the term of a typical franchise agreement.

There are no limits upon the nature and extent of fees and the term of a typical franchise agreement.

III.   Currency

If all payments under a franchise agreement must be made in immediately available U.S. Dollars, please advise as to any restrictions, reporting requirements, or regulations concerning the exchange, repatriation, or remittance of U.S. Dollars.

Pursuant to local regulations and exchange rules, such as Articles 61-63 of the *Rules of Exchange of June 2010*, repatriation by a non-resident of investment is free. To repatriate funds, a request must be submitted to the bank for transmission to the Central Bank (*Banque de la République du Burundi*) with the following information and/or documents:

- the amount to be repatriated;

- the sales contract or any other document showing the origin of the amount to be transferred; and

- a certificate of non-indebtedness issued by the Burundi Revenue Authority (*Office Burundais des Recettes*).

Capital transfers, investments in financial markets and investments abroad by residents are subject to the approval of the Central Bank. The entry of foreign currency in the form of investment is free but must be registered.

IV.   Taxes, Tariffs, and Duties

Please do not provide any in-depth comments on tax structuring. However, please provide your general comments on the typical amount of withholding tax that would apply and whether a "gross-up" provision contained in a franchise agreement would be enforceable in your country.

Burundians tax rates are as follows:

A.   Corporate Income Tax.

The general corporate tax rate is 30%.

Burundi

B.   Dividends.

A withholding tax of 15% is levied on all dividends paid by a resident company to a resident or a non-resident.

C.   Management Fees.

A 15% withholding tax is levied on management fees.

D.   Royalties.

Any professional income earned in Burundi is taxable per month according to the following table:

Tax Bands (in Burundian Francs)		Tax rate
From	To	
0	150,000	0%
150,001	300,000	20% of the amount that exceeds BIF 150,000
300,001	more	30% of the amount that exceeds BIF 300,000

The rate of the Value Added Tax, including rent for offices is 18%.

Burundi has signed a double taxation agreement within the East African Community which includes Rwanda, Tanzania, Uganda, and Kenya. However, please note that the agreement is not yet in force. Burundi does not have a double taxation agreement with the United States.

V.   Trademarks

Please advise us as to whether there are any special requirements for granting a valid trademark license, including the use of a registered user agreement or a short trademark license agreement and any required filing of such an agreement with the trademark authorities.

The license agreement must provide for control by the licensor over the services and products of the licensee. Otherwise, according to Article 334 of *Law no. 1/13 of July 28, 2009 relating to Industrial Property in Burundi*, the Court may declare that the trademark has been abandoned by its holder. The aforementioned law does not provide that the Department of Industrial Property must validate the contract to make it applicable.

While Burundian law does not specifically provide for contractual licensing, it is possible that a license agreement containing quality-control provisions will not jeopardize rights under a trademark registration.[2]

VI.   Restrictions on Transfer

Please advise as to whether there are any restrictions (1) on a franchisor to restrict transfers in a master franchisee, any interest in a master franchisee, or the assets of the master franchisee or (2) the ability of a master franchisee to control and/or restrict transfers of a subfranchisee's rights under a master franchise agreement, interest in the subfranchisee, or the assets of the subfranchisee.

Since there is no legal framework specific to franchise agreements in Burundi, the parties may freely contract regarding provisions on restrictions on transfer in the franchise agreement.

---

[2]   Edward Fennessy and International Contributors, *Trademarks Throughout the World, Fifth Edition, Release #18 28-5*, THOMAS REUTERS/WEST (2012).

VII. Termination

Please advise us as to any laws relating to termination in your country, such as agency laws, required indemnity provisions, notice or "good cause" requirements, or other laws affecting termination of a franchise agreement. Please describe.

While there are no specific laws governing termination of franchise agreements, various provisions of Burundian law govern termination in the commercial setting including under the local labor law, and commercial law. For example, certain provisions of *Law no 1/07 of April 26, 2010 on Commercial Act* provides for an indemnity in the event of termination of an agency agreement.

Pursuant to Article 225 of *Law no 1/07 of April 26, 2010 on Commercial Act* in the following instances the indemnity will not apply:

- when the breach is provoked by the gross negligence of the commercial agent;

- when the termination is the result of the commercial agent, unless it can be justified by circumstances attributable to the mandator or if it is due to the impossibility for the agent to continue its activity because of his age, infirmity, or illness;

- when after agreeing, the commercial agent cedes to a third party its rights and contractual obligations.

Local practice indicates that the parties may avoid a franchise agreement being defined as an agency agreement in Burundi by waiving any agency relationship in the franchise agreement.

Burundi

VIII. Governing Law, Jurisdiction, and Dispute Resolution

A. Choice of Law of Foreign Jurisdiction

Please confirm whether the choice of law of a foreign jurisdiction would likely to be upheld under the law of the country, except for certain matters such as trademarks, bankruptcy, and competition matters, which we assume would be governed by the law in your country.

The choice of a law of a foreign jurisdiction law can be upheld under the laws of Burundi provided that it is not contrary to public policy principles or public law in Burundi.

Under Trademarks Article 478 of *Law no 1/13 of July 28, 2009 relating to Industrial Property in Burundi* provisions of the international industrial property treaties to which Burundi is a party shall apply to the matters governed by the law and prevail in the event of conflict with the provisions of this law.

B. International Arbitration Dispute Resolution

Please confirm that a court in your country would honor an election of international arbitration dispute resolution, and therefore refuse to hear any disputes arising under a franchise agreement.

In order to enforce a foreign judgment or arbitral award in Burundi, an exequatur of such foreign judgment or arbitral award should be applied for. The exequatur will be granted if the foreign judgment or arbitral award fulfills the following conditions:

*   the judgment or arbitral award does not contain any element which is contrary to public policy principles or public law in Burundi;

- the judgment or arbitral award is final;

- the court or tribunal that rendered the judgment or arbitral award did not obtain jurisdiction solely by reason of the plaintiff's nationality;

- due process has been observed and the defendant was given an opportunity to defend itself in the proceedings resulting in the judgment or arbitral award; and

- a copy of the judgment or arbitral award is submitted which satisfies the conditions necessary for its authenticity.

Burundi is not a signatory to the *Convention on the Recognition and Enforcement of Foreign Arbitral Awards* (the *"New York Convention"*) but has initiated procedures to become a signatory.

IX.   Non-Competition Provisions

If the franchise agreement prohibits the master franchisee from engaging in certain competitive activities during the term of the agreement, and for a 12-month period after the termination or expiration of the agreement, please comment on the enforceability of non-competition covenants in your country.

Pursuant to Article 22 of *Law no 1/06 of March 25, 2010 on the Legal Regime of Competition* a non-competition provision is valid if it is limited in scope and in time and space.

X.   Language Requirements

Does the law in your country require that a franchise agreement be translated into the local language in order to be enforceable between the parties?

It is not required that the franchise agreement be translated into the local language in order to be enforceable between parties. However, please note that it should be translated into Kirundi

Burundi

(national language) or French (official language) before instituting legal action.

XI. Other Significant Matters

Please advise as to whether there are any significant matters not addressed above of which a franchisor should be aware in connection with its entering into a franchise agreement in your country.

Brassieres et Limonaderies de Burundi S.A. - Brarudi S.A. is operating under license of the Coca-Cola Company. The agreement includes use of Coca-Cola trademarks. Landline number of Brarudi S.A. is: + 257 22215360. Web site: www.brarudi.net.

Hilton Worldwide signed a license agreement with the Opulent Group as franchisee who will operate the former Novotel as a DoubleTree by Hilton in Bujumbura, Burundi, Tel: +25722222600; +25722227606.

Burundi

Bibliography of International Franchise Resources

Kendal H. Tyre, Jr., Diana Vilmenay-Hammond, Pierce Haesung Han, Courtney L. Lindsay II, and Keri McWilliams

Nixon Peabody LLP

Washington, D.C.

I.   General International Resources

Mark Abell, Gary R. Duvall, and Andrea Oricchio Kirsh, *International Franchise Legislation* B1, ABA FORUM ON FRANCHISING (1996)

Kathleen C. Anderson and Anthony M. Stiegler, *Put Muscle in Your Marks: Enforcing Intellectual Property Rights* W14, ABA FORUM ON FRANCHISING (1995)

Richard M. Asbill and Jane W. LaFranchi, *International Franchise Sales Laws—A Survey* W7, ABA FORUM ON FRANCHISING (2005)

Jeffery A. Brimer, Alison C. McElroy, and John Pratt, *Going International: What Additional Restraints Will You Face?* W4, ABA FORUM ON FRANCHISING (2011)

Michael G. Brennan, Alexander Konigsberg, and Philip F. Zeidman, *Globetrotting: A Workshop on International Franchising* 10/W8, ABA FORUM ON FRANCHISING (1994)

Michael G. Brennan, Alexander Konigsberg, and Philip F. Zeidman, *Globetrotting: Strategies for Launching U.S. Franchisors Abroad* 2/P2, ABA FORUM ON FRANCHISING (1994)

Christopher P. Bussert and Jennifer Dolman, *Regaining Your Trademark After Abandonment or Misappropriation* W7, ABA FORUM ON FRANCHISING (2011)

Ronald T. Coleman and Linda K. Stevens, *Trade Secrets and Confidential Information: Rights and Remedies* W2, ABA FORUM ON FRANCHISING (2000)

Finola Cunningham, *Commerce Department Helps Franchisors Go Global*, in FRANCHISING WORLD 63 (Dec. 2005)

Michael R. Daigle and Alex S. Konigsberg, *Meeting Off-Shore Disclosure and Contract Requirements* F/W13, ABA FORUM ON FRANCHISING (1992)

Jennifer Dolman, Robert A. Lauer, and Lawrence M. Weinberg, *Structuring International Master Franchise Relationships for Success and Responding When Things Go Awry* W22, ABA FORUM ON FRANCHISING (2007)

Gary R. Duvall, Paul Jones, and Jane LaFranchi, *Planning for the International Enforcement of Franchise Agreements* W6, ABA FORUM ON FRANCHISING (1999)

William Edwards, *International Expansion: Do Opportunities Outweigh Challenges?* in FRANCHISING WORLD (February 2008)

George J. Eydt and Stuart Hershman, *Bringing a Foreign Franchise System to the United States* W9, ABA FORUM ON FRANCHISING (2009)

William A. Finkelstein and Louis T. Pirkey, *International Trademarks* W15, ABA FORUM ON FRANCHISING (1991)

William A. Finkelstein, *Protecting Trademarks Internationally: Current Strategies and Developments* B3, ABA FORUM ON FRANCHISING (1996)

Stephen Giles, Lou H. Jones, and Lawrence Weinberg, *Negotiating and Documenting Complex International Franchise Agreements* W21, ABA FORUM ON FRANCHISING (2006)

Steven M. Goldman, Stephen Giles, Marc Israel, and Stanley Wong, *Competition Round Up from Around the World* LB2, ABA FORUM ON FRANCHISING (2004)

David C. Gryce and E. Lynn Perry, *Trademarks and Copyrights in the International Arena* 6/W4, ABA FORUM ON FRANCHISING (1993)

Kenneth S. Kaplan, Andrew P. Loewinger, and Penelope J. Ward, *System Standards in International Franchising* W14, ABA FORUM ON FRANCHISING (2005)

Edward Levitt and Jorge Mondragon, *A Survey of International Legal Traps and How to Avoid Them—Beyond the Franchise Laws* W20, ABA FORUM ON FRANCHISING (2007)

Ned Levitt, Kendal H. Tyre, and Penny Ward, *The Impossible Dream: Controlling Your International Franchise System* W4, ABA FORUM ON FRANCHISING (2010)

Michael K. Lindsey and Andrew P. Loewinger, *International (Non-U.S.) Franchise Disclosure Requirements* W9, ABA FORUM ON FRANCHISING (2002)

Andrew P. Loewinger and John Pratt, *Recent Changes and Trends in International Franchise Laws* W4, ABA FORUM ON FRANCHISING (2008)

Andrew P. Loewinger and Thomas M. Pitegoff, *Avoiding the Long Arm of the Law in International Franchising: Issues and Approaches* W8, ABA FORUM ON FRANCHISING (1995)

Craig J. Madson and Katherine C. Spelman, *Similarity and Confusion in the Intellectual Property Arena* W11, ABA FORUM ON FRANCHISING (1997)

13

Christopher A. Nowak, John Pratt, and Carl E. Zwisler, *Franchising Internationally with Countries with Opaque Legal Systems* W20, ABA FORUM ON FRANCHISING (2006)

E. Lynn Perry and John L. Sullivan Jr., *Trademark Compliance and Enforcement Techniques* E/W12, ABA FORUM ON FRANCHISING (1992)

Marcel Portmann, *Franchising Sector Proves Global Reach*, in FRANCHISING WORLD (January 2007)

John Pratt and Luiz Henrique O. do Amaral, *Civil Law for Common Law Practitioners (or How to Draft an Agreement for Use Overseas)* W4, ABA FORUM ON FRANCHISING (2002)

Kirk W. Reilly, Robert F. Salkowski and Geoffrey B. Shaw, *Determining the Rules of Engagement in Litigation Here and Abroad* W5, ABA FORUM ON FRANCHISING (2008)

Catherine Riesterer and Frank Zaid, *Basics of International Franchising* L/B2, ABA FORUM ON FRANCHISING (1997)

W. Andrew Scott and Christopher N. Wormald, *Stranger in a Strange Land: Contrasting Franchising in International Expansion* W2, ABA FORUM ON FRANCHISING (2003)

Donald Smith and Erik Wulff, *International Franchising: The Unraveling of an International Franchise Relationship* 15/W13, ABA FORUM ON FRANCHISING (1993)

Frank Zaid, Pamela Mills, and Michael Santa Maria, *Essential Issues in International Franchising* LB/1, ABA FORUM ON FRANCHISING (2001)

II.   African Resources

Joyce G. Mazero and J. Perry Maisonneuve, *Franchising in the Middle East and North Africa* W2, ABA FORUM ON FRANCHISING (2009)

Kendal H. Tyre, Jr. and Diana Vilmenay-Hammond, *Franchise World: A Burgeoning Middle Class Spurs Franchise Investment in Africa*, MINORITY BUSINESS ENTREPRENEUR (November 2012)

Kendal H. Tyre, Jr., *IP Protection May Promote Additional Franchise Growth in Africa*, NIXON PEABODY LLP: FRANCHISING BUSINESS & LAW ALERT (September 2012)

Kendal H. Tyre, Jr., *Market Potential for Franchising in Africa*, NIXON PEABODY LLP: FRANCHISING BUSINESS & LAW ALERT (June 2011)

Kendal H. Tyre, Jr. and Courtney L. Lindsay, II, *Continued Growth of Franchising in Africa*, NIXON PEABODY LLP: FRANCHISE LAW ALERT (April 2013)

Kendal H. Tyre, Jr. and Courtney L. Lindsay, II, *Pan African Franchise Federation Holds Inaugural Meeting*, NIXON PEABODY LLP: AFRICA ALERT (June 2013)

Kendal H. Tyre, Jr. and Courtney L. Lindsay, II, *White House Encouraging Private Investment and Transparency in Sub-Saharan Africa*, NIXON PEABODY LLP: AFRICA ALERT (August 2012)

Kendal H. Tyre, Jr. and Diana Vilmenay-Hammond, *African Economic Growth Impacts Franchising on the Continent*, NIXON PEABODY LLP: FRANCHISE LAW ALERT (July 2012)

Kendal H. Tyre, Jr. and Diana Vilmenay-Hammond, *Franchising in Africa*, in FRANCHISING WORLD (August 2013)

John Sotos and Sam Hall, *African Franchising: Cross-Continent Momentum*, in FRANCHISING WORLD (June 2007)

A.   Angola

João Afonso Fialho, *Franchising in Angola*, in FRANCHISING IN AFRICA: LEGAL AND BUSINESS CONSIDERATIONS 91-105 (Kendal H. Tyre, Jr. & Diana Vilmenay-Hammond eds. 2012)

B.   Botswana

Bonzo Makgalemele, *Franchising in Botswana*, in FRANCHISING IN AFRICA: LEGAL AND BUSINESS CONSIDERATIONS 107-117 (Kendal H. Tyre, Jr. & Diana Vilmenay-Hammond eds. 2012)

C.   Cape Verde

João Afonso Fialho, *Franchising in Cape Verde*, in FRANCHISING IN AFRICA: LEGAL AND BUSINESS CONSIDERATIONS 119-132 (Kendal H. Tyre, Jr. & Diana Vilmenay-Hammond eds. 2012)

D.   Egypt

Girgis Abd El-Shahid, *Franchising in Eqypt*, in FRANCHISING IN AFRICA: LEGAL AND BUSINESS CONSIDERATIONS 133-142 (Kendal H. Tyre, Jr. & Diana Vilmenay-Hammond eds. 2012)

A. Safaa El Din El Oteifi, *Egypt*, in INTERNATIONAL FRANCHISING EGY/1 (Dennis Campbell gen. ed. 2011)

E.   Ethiopia

Yohannes Assefa and Biset Beyene Molla, *Franchising in Ethiopia*, in FRANCHISING IN AFRICA: LEGAL AND BUSINESS CONSIDERATIONS 143-157 (Kendal H. Tyre, Jr. & Diana Vilmenay-Hammond eds. 2012)

Kendal H. Tyre, Jr., Yohannes Assefa and Getachew Mengistie Alemu, *New Intellectual Property Regulation Requires Scramble to Protect Marks in Ethiopia*, NIXON PEABODY LLP: AFRICA ALERT (October 2013)

F.   Ghana

Divine K.D. Letsa and Hawa Tejansie Ajei, *Franchising in Ghana*, in FRANCHISING IN AFRICA: LEGAL AND BUSINESS CONSIDERATIONS 159-167 (Kendal H. Tyre, Jr. & Diana Vilmenay-Hammond eds. 2012)

G. Libya

Kendal H. Tyre, Jr. & Diana Vilmenay-Hammond, *First U.S. Franchise Opens in Libya*, NIXON PEABODY LLP: AFRICA ALERT (August 2012)

H. Mozambique

Diogo Xavier da Cunha, *Franchising in Mozambique*, in FRANCHISING IN AFRICA: LEGAL AND BUSINESS CONSIDERATIONS 169-182 (Kendal H. Tyre, Jr. & Diana Vilmenay-Hammond eds. 2012)

I. Nigeria

Theo Emuwa and Bimbola Fowler-Ekar, *Franchising in Nigeria*, in FRANCHISING IN AFRICA: LEGAL AND BUSINESS CONSIDERATIONS 183-198 (Kendal H. Tyre, Jr. & Diana Vilmenay-Hammond eds. 2012)

Kendal H. Tyre, Jr. and Theo Emuwa, *Nigerian Franchising: Making Your Way Through the Thicket*, NIXON PEABODY LLP: FRANCHISE LAW ALERT (June 2005)

J. South Africa

Eugene Honey, *Franchising and the New Consumer Protection Bill*, BOWMAN GILFILLAN (March 2008)

Eugene Honey, *Franchising and the Consumer Protection Bill*, BOWMAN GILFILLAN (May 2008)

Eugene Honey, *Pitfalls and Difficulties with the CPA*, ADAMS & ADAMS (March 2013)

Eugene Honey, *Disclosure is Compulsory*, ADAMS & ADAMS (May 2013)

Eugene Honey and Wim Alberts, *Fundamental Consumer Rights: The Right to Equality*, BOWMAN GILFILLAN (March 2009)

Eugene Honey and Wim Alberts, *The Reach of the Consumer Protection Bill: The Final*, BOWMAN GILFILLAN (March 2009)

Eugene Honey, *South Africa*, in GETTING THE DEAL THROUGH: FRANCHISE (2013) 172-178 (Philip F. Zeidman ed. 2013)

Taswell Papier, *Franchising in South Africa*, in FRANCHISING IN AFRICA: LEGAL AND BUSINESS CONSIDERATIONS 199-224 (Kendal H. Tyre, Jr. & Diana Vilmenay-Hammond eds. 2012)

Kendal H. Tyre, Jr., *A New Legal Landscape for Franchising in South Africa*, NIXON PEABODY LLP: FRANCHISING BUSINESS & LAW ALERT (September 2009)

K.   Tunisia

Yessine Ferah, *Franchising in Tunisia*, in FRANCHISING IN AFRICA: LEGAL AND BUSINESS CONSIDERATIONS 225-245 (Kendal H. Tyre, Jr. & Diana Vilmenay-Hammond eds. 2012)

Kendal H. Tyre, Jr., Diana Vilmenay-Hammond, and Yessine Ferah, *New Franchise Legislation in Tunisia*, NIXON PEABODY LLP: FRANCHISE LAW ALERT (September 2010)

L.   Zambia

Mabvuto Sakala, *Franchising in Zambia*, in FRANCHISING IN AFRICA: LEGAL AND BUSINESS CONSIDERATIONS 247-255 (Kendal H. Tyre, Jr. & Diana Vilmenay-Hammond eds. 2012)

4845-5089-6926.3

www.ingramcontent.com/pod-product-compliance
Lightning Source LLC
Chambersburg PA
CBHW052125230326
41598CB00080B/4428

* 9 780615 994628 *